Date Due

MAR 1 3			
NOV 1 8			

Demco 38-297

Battle Ready

Raintree OSPREY PUBLISHING

Civil War State Troops

Philip Katcher • Illustrated by Ronald Volstad

This American edition first published in 2003 by Raintree, a division of
Reed Elsevier Inc., Chicago, Illinois, by arrangement with Osprey Publishing
Limited, Oxford, England.

For information, address the publisher:
Raintree, 100 N. LaSalle, Suite 1200, Chicago, IL 60602

First published 1987
Under the title *Men-at-Arms 190: American Civil War Armies (4) State Troops*
By Osprey Publishing Limited, Elms Court, Chapel Way, Botley,
Oxford, OX2 9LP
© 1987 Osprey Publishing Limited
All rights reserved.

ISBN 1-4109-0121-1

03 04 05 06 07   10 9 8 7 6 5 4 3 2 1

Author: Philip Katcher
Illustrator: Ron Volstad
Printed in China through World Print Ltd.

Author's note
The uniforms described in this book are variations from regulation US Army
and Confederate patterns.
    A word on spellings: in the 1860s, as some of the quotations in this book
make clear, Americans spelled the color both 'grey' and 'gray'.

Artist's note
Readers may care to note that the original paintings from which the color
plates in this book were prepared are available for private sale. all reproduction
copyright whatsoever is retained by the Publishers. All enquiries should be
addressed to:

    Model Emporium
    700 North Johnson
    Suite N.,
    El Cajon, CA 92020
    California
    USA

CONTENTS

CIVIL WAR STATE TROOPS

INTRODUCTION

"The War Between the States" is the term used for the American Civil War throughout much of the South even today. While it was actually a war fought between two central governments, many men on both sides – not just the South – felt that they were serving their states as much, if not more, than their central governments. Many of the states agreed, the state governments raising their own units, commissioning their officers, and supplying their men.

Indeed, many of the units that fought the Civil War were supplied in large part by their own states rather than by the central government's quartermasters. New York, for example, on the Northern side, had its own state uniforms which it provided to many of its regiments in the Union Army. On the Southern side, North Carolina also had its own dress regulations and its own factories producing uniforms and equipment, and imported additional uniforms for its troops serving with the Confederacy. Other states, too, had their own dress regulations and supplied their troops with unique uniforms. To a lesser extent, all the states – especially in 1861, when the two central governments were unable to meet the needs of all the volunteers – provided uniforms, weapons, and accoutrements for their own men.

These rarely conformed to the regulations of the Union or Confederate Armies. Colors were often different: many Northern states provided grey uniforms throughout the war, while a good number of Southern units wore blue.

A number of US units were raised in Southern states from among both white and black Union supporters, mostly towards the latter half of the war. A number of regiments were also raised in Western states and territories such as California, Utah, Colorado, and Washington. The Southern Union regiments were supplied by the US government, while some of the Western ones received state-issued supplies as well as US Army

Members of pre-war volunteer units, both North and South, wore elaborate versions of the US Army uniform in a wide variety of colors. This unknown volunteer wears a uniform that typically could have been worn either by a Northerner or Southerner – a stock shako with a standard, not unique, cap badge; apparently a dark blue coat with sky blue trim and epaulettes, with white fringe, and three rows of buttons; sky blue or grey trousers with a stripe down each leg; and a two-piece state belt plate. (Author's collection)

issue. Apart from some volunteer units, however, both categories generally wore standard US Army uniforms, and carried US Army weapons and accoutrements.

A typical volunteer camp of an unknown unit from the North or South. Old men, women, and children are visiting; the tents show no wear; and men are all neatly clad in dark blue forage caps, grey uniforms or shell jackets with shoulder straps, and grey trousers. Such a scene could have taken place near almost every town in America in early 1861. (David Scheinmann collection)

Many unique state uniforms were among the rarest of Civil War uniforms, since they were made in relatively small quantities for relatively small units. Yet they *were* worn, and their wearers played an important part in the Civil War. The uniforms themselves can be seen in the photographs in this book – yet the photographs show more than just uniforms, accoutrements, and weapons: look at the faces, too. These are the men of the Civil War; this is the real face of that war.

ALABAMA

Alabama's troops formed what the state called the "Alabama Volunteer Corps." Its uniforms, according to General Orders No. 1, issued March 28, 1861, included dark blue frock coats, cadet grey wool pants (both trimmed "as prescribed for the Confederate states service") and US Military Academy-style shakos. These were to have "the letters A.V.C.... to be placed on the cap below the eagle." Such letters were noted as being worn by Alabamians in Virginia in 1861. Woolen overcoats of jeans material lined with "heavy checked or striped osnaburg" were also to be issued. Shirts were usually brown. The state also ordered 10,000 black felt

hats with the brims "looped and buttoned on the left side."

Sgt. Crawford Jackson, 6th Alabama Infantry Regiment, wrote in July 1863 that he wore "a black broad cloth coat, Alabama staff buttons, cut and trimmed in regulation style, a pair of grey trousers and slouch hat," indicating that the AVC uniform lasted in some form at least until that date.

Grey soon became the most common Alabama coat color, however. On August 31, 1861, Governor Andrew B. Moore issued a circular in the *Montgomery Weekly Advertiser* that spelled out exactly what the state uniform should be. It included grey wool jackets made with seven brass military buttons down the front; a double thick standing collar lined with osnaburg; a strap on each shoulder running from the shoulder seam to where it buttoned at the neck; and two belt straps, one on each side of the jacket, five inches long, buttoned at the top and sewn into the jacket bottom over the side seam. Trousers were also to be of grey wool.

A grey wool overcoat was also described. This also had seven brass military buttons down the front in a single row. A detachable cape was to be attached to the collar by six hooks and eyes. The cape had a single row of five small brass military buttons down the front, and was lined with checked or striped osnaburg. Two straps on the back waistline, hidden by the cape, adjusted the waist size. The state also wanted "shirts of flannel, or checked or striped cotton; drawers of woolen, or cotton flannel, or stout osnaburgs; woolen socks; gloves, shoes, and blankets."

By the end of 1861 Alabama had acquired 7,416 complete uniforms, 2,974 greatcoats, 2,412 blankets, and some 3,000 pairs of shoes. An additional 1,532 uniforms, 900 greatcoats, 1,644 pairs of cotton drawers, 1,082 pairs of shoes, 607 blankets, and 83 pairs of gloves were acquired in the first quarter of 1862. By March 1862, however, the Confederate government was able to supply Alabama's soldiers, and thereafter the state restricted its activities to clothing reserve and local militia units.

State issue buttons: *top row, from left*, Massachusetts and Mississippi; *second row*, both North Carolina variations; *third row*, New York and Pennsylvania; *bottom row*, South Carolina and Virginia. (Author's collection)

Following the Zouave craze of 1861, a number of 1861 volunteer units also called themselves "Zouaves," apparently wearing some variation of that distinctive dress. These included the Alabama Zouaves (Law's Company), the Eufaula Zouaves (Co. K, 15th Alabama Infantry Regiment), and the Tallapoosa Zouaves (Smith's Company). Their dress was extremely short lived.

Alabama issued belt and cartridge box plates (the latter being the size of Mexican–American War US Army belt plates) which were copies of the US oval plate, but stamped with the Roman letters "AVC." These letters also appeared on brass buttons over a US Army-style eagle. Pre-war buttons with the state seal were also issued, though much more rarely. Small numbers of pre-war belt plates (but no box plates), resembling the US oval plate but with the state seal stamped on them, were also issued. There was some issue of uncommon rectangular cast plates and two-piece sword belt plates bearing the state seal as a design.

After 1862, when the M1841 rifles and M1842 muskets that had originally been supplied by the US War Department had all been issued, Alabama contracted for weapons. Contracted longarms were to be copies of the M1841 "Mississippi" rifle, and were made by Dickson, Nelson, & Co., who provided at least 645 rifles; J. P. Murray, who produced at least 262; Davis & Bozeman; and L. G. Sturdivant. James Conning Jr. made copies of the US M1840 light artillery saber for the state, while other edged weapons purchased by Alabama included pikes and knives.

ARKANSAS

Arkansas issued no state-wide dress regulations, although it did require staff militia officers to wear US Army uniforms after January 1861. Evidence indicates that grey jackets and battle-shirts were the most common state-issued or initial volunteer dress. This lack of uniformity caused each Arkansas soldier to wear a yellow flannel stripe on his left shoulder, according to the *Rock Island Register* of September 11, 1861.

Several examples exist of a stamped, lead-backed US oval-type belt plate with a state seal, but these were apparently quite rare. Buttons with the Arkansas seal were made in New Orleans during the war. There is also a known regimental button with a five-pointed star in the center, over which is "2D ARK," with "REGT" on the bottom right, and on the bottom left "CSA."

CONNECTICUT

In 1851 Connecticut issued dress regulations that closely followed those of the US Army of that time, save for the use of state buttons and cap badges. While this uniform was obsolete in 1861, some of its features survived well into the Civil War. Companies A and B of most Connecticut infantry regiments, for example, were rifle companies and wore green trim on their uniforms, while the rest were "regimental companies."

Company Quartermaster Sergeant Archibald Johnston, a native of Glasgow, Scotland, wears the uniform of The British Guard, a local defense force that helped defend Mobile, Alabama. Johnston, who had moved to Alabama in 1856, originally joined the 3rd Alabama Infantry Regiment, but received a medical discharge from that unit in May 1862. Thereafter, he joined the local unit. He was captured in the fall of Mobile on April 12, 1865. His uniform appears to be grey with black trim edged – on cuffs, trouser stripes, and chevrons – in sky blue or white. (Mrs. Ernest Brown collection)

The state provided the first clothing, accoutrements, and arms issues to its volunteer regiments up to and including 1864, unlike most other states. The 1st, 2nd, and 3rd Connecticut Infantry Regiments received trousers and coats made of blue satinet, a cheap blend of interwoven wool and cotton, and grey satinet overcoats. These uniforms were generally worn out a couple of months after their issue. When the 1st Regiment returned home after its three months' enlistment was up, its men, who had fought at Bull Run, paraded through the streets of New Haven wearing trousers made of blankets, and even captured Confederate Zouave uniforms.

However, after April 1862 the state's complete initial issue was that of the US Army, without any of the unusual units, such as Chasseurs or Zouaves, which other states organized. This is not to say, though, that everything went perfectly. The 9th Infantry Regiment, for example, an Irish unit, received uniforms made of shoddy, also called "flocked material," which fell apart with the first heavy rain. Moreover, even the better-supplied state three-year regiments reported that their first uniforms were poorly cut and badly stitched, falling apart within a month.

Connecticut's buttons bore the state coat of arms, three vines with three clusters of grapes each, over the motto "QUI TRANSTULIT SUSTINET." The same insignia had been used on the dress shakos of the 1851 regulations, although these shakos did not see Civil War use. Connecticut's staff officers wore the silver Old English letters "C.M." as their cap badge.

A heavily industrialized state, Connecticut was able to buy many of the weapons they needed from local small arms companies – including the Colt Fire Arms Company. During the war the state acquired 2,085 Springfield rifled muskets, 5,792 rifled muskets from Whitney, 5,809 P1858 Enfield rifled muskets, and 4,500 M1854 Austrian 0.54-cal. rifled muskets for its infantry. In addition, it acquired Sharps breechloaders for its 1st, 2nd and 4th Infantry Regiments; M1855 rifled muskets for the 1st, 2nd, and 5th Infantry Regiments; M1842 muskets for the 3rd and 4th Infantry Regiments, and M1855 rifles with sword bayonets for the 5th Infantry Regiment. Generally speaking, Connecticut's volunteer infantry regiments were better supplied than most, with Sharps breechloaders provided for most regiments' Companies A and B, and rifled muskets for the rest.

DELAWARE AND THE DISTRICT OF COLUMBIA

Both Delaware's and the District of Columbia's contributions to the Union Army were provided for (except for an issue of M1855 rifled muskets by Delaware to its 1st Infantry Regiment) by the US government. Neither the state nor the District had a unique belt plate insignia. Delaware made staff buttons with the state coat of arms during this period; the District did not.

FLORIDA

Standard Confederate-type uniforms, with a larger than usual number of plain shirts and straw hats being worn in tropical areas, appear to have been the norm for Floridians. The state was relatively

This youth wears the insignia adopted for the commissary sergeant of the 20th Connecticut Regiment – an insignia used, apparently, by other Connecticut regiments as well. The plain frock coat without regulation trim also seems to have been common among Connecticut's infantrymen. (Author's collection)

thinly populated, and the militia had fallen into disorder before the war. Florida did supply its Confederate troops from November 1861 through to 1864, but only in small part. Throughout 1863, for example, it supplied only 169 "undyed woolen blouse coats," with another 362 being supplied in 1864. A total of 809 "undyed woolen pants" were supplied in 1863; 1,040 were supplied the next year. Otherwise, the state supplied small quantities of undyed woolen shirts, cotton shirts, cotton underwear, cotton socks, and 700 pairs of shoes in 1864, along with blankets, scarfs, and gloves.

Buttons bearing the design of a six-pointed star with a rose wreath over the word "FLORIDA" were made in Montgomery, Alabama, during the war. Pre-war buttons with an early state seal featuring an American eagle over a cactus plant within a semicircle of 13 stars also appear to have been used by Florida troops.

GEORGIA

Most officers from Georgia – which does not seem to have printed state dress regulations – wore copies of the 1861 US Army uniform. James Cooper Nisbet, Co. H, 21st Georgia Infantry Regiment, recalled that in 1861 each man in his company was "uniformed in gray," while "the lieutenants were uniformed in home-made blue jeans. My uniform was of a regular United States Army blue, tailor-made, a present (with my sword and belt) from my sister…"

Most enlisted men wore jackets, although frocks were worn in some companies organized before the war. On August 21, 1861, Pvt. Henry Graves, 3rd Georgia Infantry Regiment, wrote home: "I wish Ma could send me a coat; let her make it of that gray woolen cloth she once made my hunting coat from… It must be a jacket, buttoning all the way up in front, with a short collar designed to stand up, buttons either brass or silver, oval shape, nearly half inch in diameter; put a short piece of white tape ¼ inch wide upon the shoulder, running from front to back. Let it be warm; pockets inside and on both sides."

Actually, the 3rd was typical of Georgia's 1861 regiments in that the uniforms varied by company, from the "buff-colored" Georgia kersey of Company F, to the red jackets and blue-black trousers with a white stripe, and "German fatigue caps" of

Private D. R. Cessar, Company E, 1st Local Troops, Georgia Infantry, wears a plain grey frock coat with apparently black trim on the odd breast pockets, around the flap over the pocket used to carry percussion caps, and around each cuff – a variation of a Georgia state uniform. Cessar's company was formed around draft-exempt workers of the Forest City Foundry in Augusta, and saw action during Sherman's campaign in that state. (Lee Joyner collection)

Company E. All the other companies wore grey uniforms, however, with black trim on them in Companies C, H, and K; green trim in Company A; and red trim in Company B. Grey was, state-wide, the most common jacket color, with 16 companies nicknamed the "Grays" raised, against only nine of "Blues." Of course, both grey and blue coats were worn in other companies, too.

Georgia did maintain its own "State Army," which included two infantry regiments, one rifle battalion, one cavalry battalion, and one artillery battalion. According to General Orders No. 4, issued February 15, 1861, its troops were to wear Georgia cadet grey frock coats and trousers, while the officers wore dark blue frock coats and trousers. Infantrymen had black patches on their standing coat collars, while artillerymen wore orange piping and trouser stripes. Blue flannel sack coats were to be worn for fatigues. US Army rank insignia were to be worn.

Besides a State Army, Georgia authorized a State Navy in January 1861. Its officers were to wear US Navy officers' uniforms with state buttons. "For the men the uniform will be… Red Shirt (flannel) with sky blue falling collar edged with white and anchor at corners; and sky blue cuffs with such other insignia on arms or elsewhere as may be usual. The trousers will be the usual Navy dark blue, and the cap a Seaman's Cap, dark blue or such other color as your men prefer (without visor) and drawn by ribbon at the side in sailor fashion." The State Navy was merged into the Confederate Navy in March 1861, probably before too many of its men received regulation uniforms.

Georgia also assisted the Confederate Army in clothing its natives, some 25,000 to 30,000 of whom were in the main army by the end of 1864. These uniforms were probably the typical Confederate plain grey jackets and trousers. On January 27, 1865, Confederate Quartermaster-General A. R. Lawton reported that "Georgia … has issued within the past year as follows: 26,795 jackets, 28,808 pairs of pants, 37,657 pairs of shoes, 7,504 blankets, 24,952 shirts, 24,168 pairs of drawers and 23,024 pairs of socks…"

The standard Georgia belt plate, apparently mostly produced before the war, was an oval, lead-backed brass plate like the US oval plate but bearing the state coat of arms. A number of these were also made into cartridge box plates. A much rarer plate was a cast brass rectangle bearing the coat of arms. A mounted man's two-piece plate was the most common sword belt plate, and this also had the state coat of arms on its "male" part. Buttons also bore the state coat of arms.

Georgia set up its own armory in the state penitentiary at Milledgeville. There, from early in 1862, some 125 M1841 "Mississippi" rifles were said to be produced every month. These were marked "GA. ARMORY" over the date on the rear of the lockplate. Saber bayonets were also made at Milledgeville. Georgia is, however, most noted for its pikes, 5,000 of which were found in storage when Milledgeville was captured on November 22, 1864. At the same time the Union troops who captured the armory also found 2,300 "smooth-bore muskets, .69 caliber," which were probably M1842 muskets.

Newspaper wood-block engravings, while inevitably somewhat distorted, were copied line for line from eyewitness sketches, and those which are the work of skilled artists are useful references. In this study, Colonel Lew Wallace (wearing a white havelock) and members of his 11th Indiana Volunteer Infantry Regiment are seen in the field in Western Virginia, August 1861. All except for the field-grade officer at the right are wearing the regiment's grey Zouave-style uniform. (Author's collection)

Indiana volunteers bury their dead after the Battle of Rich Mountain, July 1861; note the state-issued slouch hats and waist-length jackets. (Author's collection)

ILLINOIS

The only state regulation on dress in use in Illinois at the outbreak of the Civil War was a requirement that officers could wear uniforms "similar" to those worn by US Army officers. The state did not, however, have a unique state uniform for its Civil War troops. It was hoped that the US government

could uniform and equip all the state's volunteers from the beginning. This was not to be the case; and the first Illinois infantry volunteers received a state-provided issue of grey shirts, blue caps, and red blankets worn horseshoe-style. More complete uniforms were ordered from New York, arriving in May 1861. These included "a jacket and pants of course grey cloth, blue Zouave cap, and substantial shoes." The clothes were made of poor quality wool – known as "shoddy" – and wore out quickly.

Ten more infantry regiments were authorized on May 2, 1861, and these wore clothing provided by their hometowns. Most of these uniforms included grey or blue jackets and trousers. The state itself contracted for additional uniforms on June 12, 1861, so that each of its volunteers would receive "a blue or gray round jacket and pantaloons of the US Army pattern, two flannel shirts, two pairs of drawers, two pairs of socks, one pair of brogan shoes." Most of these uniforms were grey, due to a lack of blue cloth. Plain grey frock coats or jackets, with some blue jackets, grey trousers, and grey broad-brimmed hats (turned up on one side, with a plain brass button over a red, white, and blue cockade) were issued to the 13th to 22nd Illinois Volunteer Infantry Regiments from this contract. The 7th to 12th Regiments, in the 1st Brigade of Illinois Volunteers, received grey coats (edged in blue for infantry, red for artillery) with short skirts; grey trousers, and grey broad-brimmed hats. "The fatigue suit is a shirt, pantaloons and Zouave cap in a firm hickory cloth," noted the *Chicago Tribune* in April 1861.

At the same time, the 1st to 5th Cavalry Regiments received red shirts and "dark blue reinforced pants" as their initial issue, after which they received "jackets and black hats." By mid-1862 they, too, were clothed by the US government in regulation dress.

In September 1862 Illinois turned over all its purchased clothing and equipment to the US Quartermaster. This included 25,044 dress hats, 59,172 caps, 3,432 havelocks, 19,046 dress coats, 64,412 jackets (obviously the most common state-issued type of coat), 11,072 fatigue shirts, 112,287 pairs of trousers, 21,878 pairs of boots, 93,148 pairs

Pierre G. T. Beauregard, soon to be a Confederate general, wears the all dark blue uniform of a colonel of engineers in the Louisiana State Army in 1861. The trouser cord is gold; shoulder straps are gold on a dark blue ground; the cap badge has a castle within a gold wreath. (Author's collection)

Simon Bolivar Buckner, who commanded Kentucky's volunteer units before joining the Confederate forces, wears that state's officers' uniform. Many of these uniforms were worn by Confederate Kentuckians and, indeed, apparently by other Confederate generals. (David Scheinmann collection)

volunteers flocked to the colors. The state quickly advertised for uniforms from private contractors, to include "coat and pants of strong, cheap woolen goods ... flannel shirts ... gray blankets." The coats were to be "jackets [which were] to be wadded in the breast, to be lined, etc. ... with inside pocket, with nine regulation buttons in front and two on each sleeve." Satinet was to be used to uniform three regiments, and jeans material another two. Hats were "to be light colored, taper crown, felt wool hats to be looped up at each side." Apart from the color they must have looked like the US Army dress hat.

Essentially, as produced, the 6th and 7th Infantry Regiments (the numbers 1 to 5 were reserved for the Mexican–American War Indiana regiments) wore short grey jackets and grey trousers with blue flannel shirts. The 8th wore light blue short jackets and trousers, possibly trimmed with dark blue. The 9th wore grey satinet jackets and trousers. The 10th probably wore plain light blue jeans, jackets and trousers. This uniform was replaced by grey uniforms trimmed in black in September 1861. All of them wore the grey felt hats.

The 11th wore Zouave-style jackets and trousers as their first uniforms. Their first commander, Lew Wallace, recalled later: "Our outfit was of the tamest gray twilled goods – not unlike homemade jeans – a visor cap, French in pattern, its top of red cloth not larger than the palm of one's hand; a blue flannel shirt with open neck;

A white cotton duck haversack with bone buttons. Both the inside of the haversack and the detachable food bag that buttons inside it are marked "STATE OF MASS./ INSPECTED/ACCEPTED." (Author's collection)

of shoes, 72,866 overcoats, 95,967 wool blankets, 20,367 rubber or "enameled" blankets, 35,223 knapsacks, 45,925 haversacks, and 54,740 canteens. The state nevertheless continued to issue clothing to its troops, equipping all its infantry regiments up to the 131st with uniform jackets rather than frock coats.

No buttons, belt plates, or cap badges with special Illinois insignia are known to have been issued.

Illinois armed its infantrymen with state-purchased weapons including Springfield rifled muskets and 0.69 caliber US and Prussian muskets. The state also purchased Sharps carbines and Colt revolvers for its mounted men.

INDIANA

When the Civil War broke out there were only six volunteer companies active within Indiana. Immediately, however, six regiments-worth of

a jacket Greekish in form, edged with narrow binding, the red scarcely noticeable; breeches baggy, but not petticoated; button gaiters connecting below the knees with the breeches, and strapped over the shoe." In December 1861 this uniform was replaced by a blue one, which Wallace wrote included a "dark blue jacket, and sky blue Zouave pants with shirts." Cpl. Sylvester Bishop wrote home that the new jackets "are black with a blue front that buttons up close, which makes it look like a vest."

Regiments raised subsequently wore standard US Army uniforms issued by the Federal government. However, broad-brimmed black hats were widely issued to and worn by Indiana soldiers, as were blue fatigue jackets of the same general description as the first regulation grey jackets.

Indiana troops wore no special state cap badges, buttons, or belt plates. The state's first regiments were issued M1842 muskets; later, Indiana acquired 40,000 P1853 Enfield rifled muskets, and about half the state's volunteers received these weapons, while the rest received various US-made longarms. Cavalrymen received Wesson breech-loading carbines and, probably, Lefaucheux revolvers.

IOWA

Iowa had been apathetic about supporting an active militia before the Civil War, and was therefore unprepared to equip its volunteers in 1861. The governor quickly sent an agent to Chicago to buy cloth for 1,500 uniforms, to be made up by patriotic women in the state. All he could find in sufficient supply was a grey satinet; this was deemed acceptable, and the material was purchased, sent back to Iowa, and turned into uniforms.

This material was used for uniforms issued to the 1st Iowa Infantry Regiment. Volunteers from Davenport had uniforms made which included loose-fitting blouses, like shirts, worn over the trousers, with green collars; and dark grey trousers with a stripe down each leg. Officers had black felt hats, turned up on the side with a red, white, and blue tin cockade. Volunteers from Keokut and Burlington had much the same uniform, except that the trim was of red flannel. These uniforms were totally worn out after the Battle of Wilson's Creek, to the extent that many of the

Colonel Charles Devens, Jr., 15th Massachusetts Infantry, wears a typical Massachusetts version of the US Army uniform, with white trim on his collar and képi, and white cords down each trouser leg. His collar is also edged with gold, and the képi has additional gold decoration. The 15th was part of the defending force that stopped Pickett's Charge and helped win the Battle of Gettysburg. (David Scheinmann collection)

soldiers wore aprons of flour sacks to hide their ragged trousers. New uniforms were ordered from a Boston contractor, including grey wool frock coats and trousers, grey wool flannel shirts, and grey felt hats. This dress, called the "state gray uniform," was issued to the 1st to 3rd Infantry Regiments; but later regiments were supplied by the Federal government with regulation Army dress, accoutrements, and weapons.

There was no unique state insignia worn on buttons, belt plates, or cap badges. Iowa was able to obtain a hodge-podge of weapons, including Austrian, Prussian, French, Belgian, and British muskets and rifles, along with M1842 muskets from the US government, all of which it issued to its volunteers.

KENTUCKY

Kentucky's volunteers of 1861, drawn from pre-war volunteer units, wore both blue and grey coats and trousers – grey being slightly more common. However, as a "neutral" state which rapidly fell into Union hands, Kentucky provided both Confederate and Union units equipped and uniformed by their respective armies rather than by the state. There were two-piece sword belt plates with the state seal on the male part; and buttons with the state motto and seal, made both in the North, possibly by the Scovil Co., and in France. Men on both sides wore these items.

LOUISIANA

"The Louisiana troops were, as a general thing, better equipped and more regularly uniformed than any others in the motley throng," wrote an observer in Richmond in 1861. However, there was no statewide uniform; and volunteer companies out West wore a red flannel stripe on their left shoulders, according to the *Rock Island Register* of September 11, 1861.

Generally, state staff officers wore dark blue copies of US Army uniforms, while various companies selected their own uniforms. Blue appears to have been the most common volunteer color in New Orleans, with ten companies of "Blues" raised, mostly in that city, among Louisiana's volunteers. There were also, statewide,

nine companies of "Grays." The grey uniforms appear to have included mostly jackets trimmed in various colors, although black was the most common color.

As one might expect from an area with traditional ties to France, a number of Zouave and Chasseur uniforms were seen among the 1861 Louisiana volunteer units. These included the Confederate States Zouaves (St. Leon Dupeire's Louisiana Infantry), the Louisiana Zouaves, and the Zouaves and Chasseurs. They all seem to have worn basically the same dress, similar to that described by a soldier of the 79th New York Infantry Regiment, who saw a member of Wheat's Battalion of Louisiana Zouaves: "His uniform attracted our attention: a Zouave cap of red, and jacket of blue, with baggy trousers made of blue and white striped material, and white leggings." The jacket was trimmed with scarlet.

There was so much blue among Louisiana uniforms in 1861 that in the First Battle of Bull Run the state's soldiers wore red armbands above their left elbows as a field sign. By early 1862, however, Gen. Richard Taylor wrote that his brigade of the 6th, 7th, 8th, and 9th Louisiana Infantry Regiments was "over three thousand strong, neat in fresh clothing of gray with white gaiters, bands playing at the head of their regiments...."

Louisiana also raised a state navy to defend the Mississippi River. Confederate Navy Capt. C. W. Read later wrote that each of Louisiana's gunboats "...had a frigate's complement of officers, and they all wore the blue uniform of the United States Navy." However, a photograph of Capt. Beverly Kennon, commander of the LSS *Governor Moore*, shows a double-breasted coat that appears to be grey, with a dark blue or black standing collar edged with a wide gold lace trim along the top and front and a narrower lace trim along the bottom. He wears a pair of shoulder straps of dark blue or black edged gold with an insignia inside, possibly that of a US Navy captain. While not shown in the photograph, the use of grey for the coat suggests grey trousers and a grey cap, possibly with a gold band like that of the US Navy.

The standard-issue Louisiana belt plate was rectangular, of lead-backed stamped brass, bearing the state insignia of a pelican feeding its young within a laurel wreath. Examples of this plate in cast brass also exist, as do two-piece buckles with the seal on the male part. The female part is often plain, without the traditional laurel wreath, although wreathed examples do exist. The state button bore the same insignia.

MAINE

There was no regulation Maine uniform. The first six volunteer infantry regiments, when raised in 1861, received state-purchased uniforms that included grey frock coats, with eight Maine buttons down the front; plain grey trousers; and plain grey forage caps. The actual colors varied from "Canada gray," through "light gray" and "dark gray," to "cadet gray." A major of the 3rd Maine Infantry Regiment recalled that when they were organized in 1861, "We were clothed in new gray uniforms, and equipped and armed, our guns were Springfield smooth-bore, muzzle-loading muskets, fixed with the common bayonet." These uniforms were replaced with regulation blue dress when they reached Washington in July. Blue uniforms were issued by the state to its 7th, 8th, and 9th Infantry Regiments, and the US government issued regulation clothing to all regiments thereafter. Wherever possible, however, Maine troops seemed to prefer dark blue trousers to regulation sky blue, wearing them whenever they got the chance.

Maine issued both buttons with the state coat of arms on them, and oval, US Army-like brass belt plates marked "VMM" (for "Volunteer Militia of Maine"). The belt plates came only in the smaller size used in the Mexican–American War, although the "VMM" cartridge box plates came in the large size then currently issued by the US Army. These plates were worn by the low-numbered Maine infantry regiments including the 10th (although the 1st Regiment received US plates), as well as by some later units whenever they were available. These plates were worn at the front as late as 1864.

Maine issued from its stores, M1855 rifles to the 1st and 6th Infantry Regiments, as well as P1858 Enfields to the 10th and 13th Infantry Regiments. M1841 rifles went to the 4th (but not enough for the whole regiment) and 7th Infantry Regiments.

The only organized force from the state of California to see action in the East was the "California 100," a company raised in California which served in the 2nd Massachusetts Cavalry. The unit wore regulation dress, except for this unique cap badge. The 2nd was organized in February 1863 and served mostly in Northern Virginia against guerrilla forces there. (James Stamatelos collection)

MARYLAND

Maryland's Union troops wore standard US Army uniforms and carried issue weapons and accoutrements. The state's approximately 25,000 men who fought in the Confederate Army were luckier than many in that they had families behind Federal lines who had access to much more material than did those living in the South, and they were therefore often better supplied from home than typical Confederates. On September 19, 1862, a 9th New York Infantry Regiment private saw the Confederate 1st Maryland Infantry Regiment on the march: "They were noticeable, at that early stage of the war, as the only organization we saw that wore the regulation Confederate gray, all the other troops having assumed a sort of revised regulation uniform of homespun butternut...."

In 1863 Maryland Confederate Gens. George H. Steuart and Bradley T. Johnston attempted to form a "Maryland Line" of state units, and gathered six Maryland infantry, artillery, and cavalry units at a camp in northern Virginia. From diggings at this site it appears that the US-type oval brass belt plate and cartridge box plate with the state seal were quite common. Two-piece sword belt plates with the state seal on the male part were also common. Union Maryland troops do not appear to have worn state plates to any great extent.

Pvt. Henry Holiday, Co. A, 2nd Maryland Infantry Battalion, CSA, was among the many who wore a cast rectangular brass belt plate, the state seal being displayed within an oval. An additional state insignia worn by Marylanders was a metal (often silver) cross *botonée* – called the "Cross of Calvert" – which was sometimes engraved with the wearer's name and unit designation, and was pinned to the left breast.

MASSACHUSETTS

Massachusetts authorized a state uniform in 1852, but these regulations were little followed by its volunteer units, who preferred their own designs. As was the case with most other states, Massachusetts was ill-prepared to clothe and equip its volunteers in 1861. According to the *Boston Daily Advertiser* of April 17, 1861, in the state's new 3rd, 4th, 6th, and 8th Infantry Regiments "each soldier is to be supplied with two woolen shirts, two pairs of stockings, one pair of boots and a Guernsey frock." This was, however, merely a stop-gap measure.

The state quickly ordered grey flannel state uniforms, including jackets for all branches, and red fezzes (later, broad-brimmed grey felt hats). In 1861 Massachusetts bought 9,884 grey infantry jackets, 1,687 cavalry and artillery jackets, 13,730 infantry frock coats, 22,774 fatigue blouses, 35,339 overcoats, 34,208 pairs of trousers, 32,763 pairs of shoes, 2,650 mounted men's boots, 18,092 fatigue caps, and 16,714 hats. They also bought 11,074 "uniform suits," including 199 Zouave uniforms.

The state grey uniforms went to the 7th, 9th, 10th, and 11th Massachusetts Volunteer Infantry Regiments. The state's 2nd and 12th Regiments started out with US Army regulation uniforms. Thereafter, grey uniforms were not acceptable to the US authorities, and the state began to issue blue regulation clothing.

Massachusetts had a button that used "the Massachusetts arms with the word Massachusetts"

for generals and the words "Mass. Vol. Militia" for other officers and enlisted men. Among officers examples were to be seen of both cast brass rectangular and two-piece brass sword belt plates bearing the state coat of arms. US regulation plates, though, were the most common type used by Massachusetts volunteers.

Sergeant Frederick A. Cline, 40th Missouri Infantry Regiment, wears the short uniform jacket so commonly issued in Western states. The otherwise plain jacket has straps on each shoulder, and "keeper" tabs on each side through which the waist belt is passed. He is armed with an M1842 musket and a Colt Navy revolver. The cap badge design is unknown; it was probably simply the regimental number. The 40th do not appear to have had a very distinguished career, most of their time was spent in garrison duty. (John Ertzgaard collection)

In 1861 Massachusetts bought 5,000 M1842 muskets, 4,000 M1841 rifles, 14,700 P1858 Enfield rifled muskets, 10,000 sets of British-made infantry accoutrements, 32,400 US-made infantry accoutrements, 1,960 M1841 riflemen's accoutrements, 285 Savage revolvers, 889 sabers, and 900 saber bayonets for its volunteers. Thereafter, the state contracted with S. Norris and W. T. Clement for 3,000 M1863 rifled muskets which were marked on the lockplate "S.N.&W.T.C./ FOR/MASSACHUSETTS."

MICHIGAN

When the Civil War began the state's quartermaster-general was ordered to have uniforms made of "blue flannel or of some suitable material of blue color." Photographs of the 2nd Michigan Volunteer Infantry Regiment show them wearing dark blue trousers and dark blue waist-length jackets with standing collars; shoulder straps that run from the shoulder seam to a small button next to the collar; and nine large buttons down the front. On August 24, 1861, Michigan's governor cabled the US Secretary of War that "the Sixth Regiment of Michigan Volunteer Infantry...will be supplied...with uniforms (of blue), undershirts, drawers, forage-caps, stockings, and shoes, and with tents, cooking utensils, haversacks, and canteens. I request that provision may be made furnishing them with arms and accoutrements." Further, he wrote, the 7th was "supplied with clothing and camp equippage similar to that furnished the Sixth Regiment." Both the 1st and 5th Regiments would receive this type of clothing as soon as it was available, and it was then "under contract and is being pressed forward with all possible dispatch." Blue uniforms thus seem to have been used by Michigan volunteers from the beginning, save for different uniforms made for a handful of volunteer companies on their initial organization; these, of course, lasted only a very short time.

Michigan troops do not seem to have worn any special state insignia. The state was able to arm its first three regiments with M1855 rifled muskets; thereafter the state's arms ran out, and a mixture of foreign-made weapons went to later regiments.

MINNESOTA

A frontier state, Minnesota clothed its first volunteers with checkered flannel shirts (mostly red, although some were blue and some had various designs printed on them), broad-brimmed black felt hats, black trousers, shoes, blankets, and woolen underwear. It was not until the summer of 1861 that the 1st Minnesota Volunteer Infantry Regiment received US Army regulation uniforms. The 2nd Regiment was also clothed by the state, but later regiments received clothing directly from the US Army. Both regiments also received M1842 muskets from the state. There was no unique state insignia worn by Minnesota volunteers.

MISSISSIPPI

Ten Mississippi prisoners of war were said to have arrived in Washington, DC, by the *Daily National Intelligencer* of July 25, 1861: "One of them is Lieut. Col. B. B. Boone, a splendid officer in appearance, though clad in rough gray cloth, trimmed in faded cotton velvet facings."

Col. Boone's uniform appears to have been that prescribed by the state's military board in January 1861: "All officers shall wear a frock coat of gray cloth, the skirt to extend from two-thirds to three-fourths of the distance from the top of the hip to the bend of the knee." Generals and field officers had two rows of buttons, seven in each row, the rows being five and a half inches apart at the top and three and a half at the bottom. Company-grade officers had one row of nine buttons. Field officers were to have black standing collars trimmed in half-inch-wide gold lace. Three small buttons were to be worn at each cuff, one at each hip, and one at each skirt end. Company officers were to have colored collars trimmed in half-inch-wide gold lace, colored cuffs, and "silk braid of the facings of the corps, running each side from the buttons, the top braid extending five inches and the bottom one two inches, and the intermediate braids graduating from one to the other."

Enlisted men were to wear coats like those of company grade officers, but with branch-of-service color worsted braid on the chest. Branch-of-service colors were unusual: crimson for infantry and riflemen, yellow for cavalry, and orange for artillery.

Typically, New Hampshire infantrymen wore forage caps decorated with their branch of service insignia, company letter, regimental number, and "NHV" for New Hampshire Volunteers. The regulation frock coat was most commonly worn, as by this member of Company E, 15th New Hampshire Infantry Regiment. The 15th was raised in early 1862 for nine months of active duty with the Army of the Potomac, seeing action at Chancellorsville. (David Scheinmann collection)

The rather odd-looking "Whipple" cap, as worn by this soldier, was issued to men from New Hampshire and New York, as well as other northeastern states: see Plate B3. The man's apparently state-issue jacket has shoulder straps trimmed in sky blue, but has no trim on the standing collar. (David Scheinmann collection)

"For fatigue, a *red* flannel shirt with a star of white on each side of the collar, for Infantry or Riflemen, a grey flannel shirt for Artillery, and *blue* for Cavalry."

Trousers were grey, with black cords being worn by generals, an inch-wide black stripe by field grade officers, and an inch-wide branch-of-service color stripe for everyone else.

Officers' epaulets were almost the same as the US Army pattern, except that a major-general wore a single gold star; a lieutenant-colonel, a gold leaf; and a major, a silver leaf. Shoulder straps bore the same insignia, on a dark blue ground for all branches of service. Non-commissioned officers wore Confederate Army style chevrons in branch-of-service colors. A half-chevron was allowed to be worn above the cuff to mark previous US military service. Major-generals were also marked by a gold star, three-quarters of an inch in diameter, on each collar; brigadier-generals wore it in silver.

Hats were black, broad-brimmed, "looped up on three sides, when on parade, to be ornamented with cord, tassel and plumes … the plumes to be made of horse hair." Major-generals had long, flowing white plumes; brigadier-generals, red plumes tipped with white; medical officers, green plumes; adjutant general's corps officers, yellow plumes; quartermaster general's department, blue plumes; ordnance corps officers, blue plumes tipped with red; and other officers and men, plumes of branch-of-service color "with a yellow metal number of their Regiments below the plume socket." Hat cords were also in branch or corps colors. While these hats appear from photographs to have been common, the plumes seem to have been but rarely worn.

All officers were to wear crimson sashes. Cravats were to be "black, light, to be worn loose." Overcoats were "for all non-commissioned officers and men... sacks made of waterproof cotton."

Judging from photographs, this uniform was not only issued in 1861, but worn for some considerable time after.

According to the 1861 orders, sword belt plates were to be, for officers, "a plain clasp of gilt or brass," and for men, "a plain brass buckle." US-type oval brass belt plates and cartridge box plates bearing the state seal of an eagle within an oval were also worn, some 2,000 of them having been made by a Massachusetts manufacturer before the war. A cast brass rectangular plate with the same design was also used.

Buttons were not described in orders, but surviving examples have a five-pointed star, with the legend "MISSISSIPPI" around the edge. Most have a block letter "I," "A," or "C" in the star's center, depending on the wearer's branch of service.

Mississippi had its own state armory which mostly converted civilian weapons to 0.58-cal. military longarms. It did produce some Maynard pattern carbines, and possibly even some rifles. The 1st Mississippi Infantry Regiment was armed with these state-made weapons. The state also converted and issued 1,000 Hall flintlock rifles to its troops.

MISSOURI

Missouri's Union troops wore standard US Army dress and carried regulation weapons and accoutrements. Her contributions to the Confederate Army were attired in so motley a fashion that Missourians had to wear a field sign – a white flannel stripe on the left shoulder – according to the September 11, 1861, *Rock Island Register*. Missourians on both sides wore US-type oval, stamped brass belt plates bearing the Roman letters "SMM," for "State of Missouri Militia," whenever they could get them.

NEW HAMPSHIRE

According to a veteran of the 2nd New Hampshire Infantry Regiment, when the unit was raised in 1861 "the uniforms were gray, the jaunty forage caps and 'spiketail' dress coats banded with red cord." The *New-Hampshire Gazette* of May 11, 1861, described the uniform as including a "gray coat and pants, gray overcoat, gray fatigue cap, two flannel shirts, one

pair of flannel drawers, one extra pair of socks, one pair of shoes, and one large camp blanket." This was what was decided upon for the state uniform when the war began, with the addition of an officer's uniform that included US Army coats and trousers (albeit with red stripes down the legs), and red képis with dark blue bands trimmed with gold.

Most New Hampshire troops from the 4th Infantry Regiment on received a revised state uniform that conformed to US Army regulations. These were described by Henry Little of the 7th New Hampshire Infantry as "'keg hats' of black felt, trimmed with feathers and brasses, dark blue dress coats, dark blue trousers, light blue overcoats, dark blue blouses, and dark blue fatigue caps, the trimmings had chevrons of light blue, except the dark blue… [chevron] on the overcoats." Generally, these forage caps were decorated by New Hampshiremen with the brass letters "NHV" on the lower edge of the crown, below the regulation bugle-horn, a regimental number within the loop, and with a company letter above that.

Another state peculiarity was an oval, US Army-type belt plate marked in Roman letters "NHSM." A cartridge box plate so marked was also issued. After about 1862, however, these were used by troops within the state, while those at the front wore US plates.

New Hampshire equipped its first two infantry regiments with M1842 muskets and the 3rd with P1858 Enfields; later regiments received their longarms directly from the US Army.

NEW JERSEY

New Jersey ordered for its first volunteers a uniform that included "a dark blue frock coat, light blue pants, and army cockade hat." These coats appear to have been made like the US Army's fatigue blouse, but with five buttons down the front instead of four. State-made or -bought uniforms were issued to New Jersey's first nine infantry regiments. The US Army equipped those raised later.

Exceptions were the 33rd and 35th New Jersey Volunteer Infantry Regiments, which received directly from the state Zouave uniforms including dark blue jackets, waistcoats, and trousers, a blue sash edged with light blue, and blue and red caps.

The state also equipped the 3rd Cavalry Regiment with a "hussar" type of uniform, based on the regulation uniform but with additional trim.

In 1863 New Jersey raised a rifle corps for home defense. This unit wore Chasseur uniforms, made usually of grey, although sometimes of blue for dress occasions; and a grey jacket, trousers and forage cap (again, sometimes blue) for fatigue wear. Officers apparently wore gold-embroidered crossed rifles, with the letters "NJ" above the cross and "RC" under it, on their caps.

Other state insignia included buttons with the state arms, and oval, US Army-type brass belt plates marked "NJ" in Roman letters. The latter are extremely rare, and do not appear to have been worn at the front.

New Jersey had a state armory in Trenton, the state capital, which produced copies of the M1861 rifled musket for its troops. The state also bought Remington army revolvers and light cavalry sabers, as well as converting flintlock muskets to percussion for its active militia.

The 3rd New Jersey Cavalry Regiment styled themselves the "1st US Hussars." Their uniform was the regulation issue, with additions in the way of braid made by the State of New Jersey: see Plate H3. The regiment, raised in the latter part of the war, had an excellent record. (Richard Carlisle collection)

This short dark blue jacket trimmed in sky blue seems to have been worn by many New Jersey infantry officers, including, as seen here, Colonel William B. Hatch of the 4th New Jersey Infantry Regiment. Colonel Hatch was killed in action at the Battle of Fredericksburg. (US Army Military History Institute)

NEW YORK

When the Federal government requested troops to put down the rebellion, New York sent 11 of its militia regiments to Washington, and called for another 30,000 volunteer militia for two years' service. These went into newly organized regiments.

New York's governor cabled the Secretary of War on June 28, 1861 that he had "already contracted for the making of 10,000 suits of uniforms with two parties, 2,500 to be delivered this week, of the best army goods, at $16.50 per suit, and for 20,000 caps, with capes and covers complete, at 75 cents." These uniforms were to conform to the state's "Act of April 16, 1861":

"That the uniform of the troops should consist:

1st. Of a jacket of dark blue army cloth, cut to flow from the waist and to fall about four inches below the belt. The coat to be buttoned with eight buttons, from the throat to the waist. The collar to be a low standing collar. The buttons are to be those of the state militia.

2nd. Of trowsers, to be made of light army blue, cut full in the leg and large around the foot...

3rd. Of an overcoat of light army blue, of the pattern worn by the US infantry...

New Jersey's Rifle Corps wore grey uniform jackets with standing collars, grey trousers, and grey képis with dark blue or black bands around them. The Corps was raised for state defense. (Author's collection)

Lieutenant-Colonel Eli K. Lyon, 43rd New York State Militia Regiment, was photographed just prior to the war in the State's 1858 regulation uniform – the standard when the war began. It is virtually the same as the US Army uniform apart from state insignia. Lyon wears a two-piece belt plate and a presentation sword. (Michael McAfee collection)

4th. Of a fatigue cap of dark blue, with a water-proof cover, to be made with a cape which will fall to the shoulder. The cover to be buttoned at the visor, and furnished with strings, so that it may be tied under the chin….

Each soldier should be provided with two canton-flannel shirts, two pair canton-flannel drawers, two pair woolen socks, one pair stout cowhide pegged shoes and one double Mackinac blanket. The board would suggest that the Commissioned officers of this force be uniformed according to the bill of dress for officers already established by the general regulations."

Therefore, on April 16, 1861, Pvt. Joseph Favill of the 71st New York Infantry Regiment noted in his diary that the unit was to report to a clothing store the next day, "there to be measured, each and all of us, for a uniform suit, to consist of dark blue jacket and sky-blue trousers. The jacket will have light blue shoulderstraps and cuffs."

This jacket, as most commonly issued to New York volunteers, was short, dark blue, with a standing collar fastened with a hook-and-eye in front, and trimmed with wide light blue piping. On jackets made later the piping was of a medium, almost blue-green color, and was thinner than the thicker cords used on the first jackets. There was a strap passing from the shoulder seam to a button next to the collar on each shoulder; these were also trimmed in light blue, as was a left-side "belt keeper" tab. Small New York state buttons were used on these. There were eight large New York state buttons in a single row down the front, although examples with seven and nine buttons are also known to have been made.

The 69th New York State Militia Regiment parades in New York upon its return from the Battle of First Bull Run. In the engraving the regimental number can clearly be seen on the slouch hat of the private holding the bouquet in the center of the front rank. See Plate G2. (Author's collection)

Major Alexander Shaler wears the uniform of the famous 7th New York State Militia Regiment, from which he resigned in June 1861. The 7th was the first regiment to reach Washington after pro-Southerners had cut its communications at the beginning of the war. (David Scheinmann collection)

trimmed in red. They were very popular items, and other units took them into use whenever possible

This private wears the Chasseur uniform adopted by the 12th New York State Militia Regiment in 1861. The dark blue uniform is trimmed with light blue; trousers are sky blue; leggings are of russet leather; and the képi is light blue with a dark blue band, white cord trim, and the brass number "12" in front. The 12th served three months' active service starting in May 1861, and behaved well in a skirmish near Martinsburg, Virginia, on July 12, before being mustered out. (David Scheinmann collection)

The jackets were lined in the breast with brown polished cotton stiffened with burlap, with dark-colored twill tape sewn over the back seams. A "slash" pocket lined in brown polished cotton was usually worn over the left breast, normally large enough to hold a small Bible or a diary. The sleeves had two small state buttons on each cuff, although they were for appearance only – the cuff could not be opened. Sleeves were lined with white muslin.

As was often the case, not enough blue material was immediately available for all the volunteers, and New York had to obtain 7,300 cadet grey "mixed satinet" jackets and trousers for many of its men. Most of these were poorly made of inferior materials and wore out quickly.

The blue state jackets were issued to the 1st to 105th New York Regiments before the US Army took over the task of providing its uniforms. Artillery regiments from the 1st to the 4th, plus a number of batteries, received the same jackets (many units were given a choice of the state jacket or US frock coat). They served as dress coats, being issued and worn until at least October 1864, when troops of the 120th New York Volunteer Infantry Regiment (which was not one of the regiments supposed to have been issued them) were photographed wearing them.

On May 16, 1863, New York issued a general order calling for a single state militia uniform. Each militia regiment could wear a dark blue jacket with nine state buttons down the front, a standing collar and pointed cuffs trimmed white. Two styles were authorized: a Chasseur style, and a "polka jacket." Trousers were "light indigo blue kersey," with edging around the pockets for those units with Chasseur jackets. Caps were dark blue képis piped in white, orange, green, or scarlet. A state coat of arms in brass under a red, white, and blue pompon was worn by enlisted men on the cap front.

Mounted units wore the US mounted jackets with dress caps or black broad-brimmed hats. These uniforms began to be issued in large quantities (5,000) in 1864.

The state coat of arms also appeared on buttons worn by officers and men. The sword belt plate for all officers, non-commissioned officers, musicians and mounted privates was "gilt, rectangular, two inches wide, with a raised bright rim; a silver wreath of laurel and palm encircling the letters 'NY' in old

The 8th New York State Militia Regiment, photographed here near Washington during the regiment's three months' active service in 1861, wore cadet grey jackets, trousers and képis with black trim. The cross belt plate worn by the soldier on the extreme right bears the insignia of a bust of Washington within a wreath. Note the full haversack with a tin cup buckled to its flap and the blanket roll worn by the soldier in the center; and the ax carried by, apparently, a pioneer. (Michael McMee collection)

English characters in silver." New York's heavy artillerymen also wore a two-piece belt plate with the Roman letters "SNY" on the male part. Enlisted foot soldiers wore US Army-style oval brass belt plates and cartridge box plates marked in Roman letters "SNY." Most of the men who enlisted for two years in 1861 wore this plate. Other units, such as the 100th Infantry Regiment, also wore them whenever they could get them, and they have been found at sites dating from 1864, indicating their use late in the war.

In 1861 New York bought or acquired 25,540 M1842 muskets, 20,397 P1858 Enfields, 5,000 0.54-cal. Austrian rifled muskets, and several thousand more US-made and imported longarms.

The 1st New York Regiment of Marine Artillery was organized to man naval guns defending the state against attack by sea, and was disbanded in 1863. Officers, like Lieutenant G. Gerrarrd shown here, wore all dark blue uniforms, with naval caps trimmed in gold with a badge of a crossed cannon and anchor. Their swords were the US Navy regulation models. The men wore blue Navy jumpers and shirts, grey trousers with red stripes, and blue forage caps, with blue jackets for cold weather. (David Scheinmann collection)

NORTH CAROLINA

In 1861 there was the usual collection of volunteer companies in various uniforms in North Carolina. There were eight companies of "Blues" and 23 of "Grays," indicating a clear preference for grey uniforms. These uniforms quickly wore out, however, and the men needed new ones.

North Carolina was unique among Southern states in that from September 20, 1861, it took over the responsibility for clothing its own troops. The state set up a clothing factory in Raleigh which made, during its one year of existence, 49,000 jackets, 68,000 pairs of trousers, 12,000 blankets, and 6,000 overcoats. The overcoats were grey "with capes lined with lindsey and stiffened with canvas." The state also issued, during the same period, 8,918 hats and 61,949 caps. The state had its own uniform regulations. On April 19, 1861, the state Adjutant General wrote to the 1st North Carolina Infantry Regiment's commander that "The gray or blue blouse will be recognized as a suitable uniform." However, on May 27, 1861, General Orders No. 1 were issued, and spelled out a much more complete uniform.

Officers were to wear frock coats, two rows of seven buttons each for field grade officers and one row of nine buttons for company grade officers. The color was "North Carolina [made] gray cloth," a grey with a brownish tinge to judge from surviving examples. Generals and staff officers were to wear dark blue coats. Rank badges were US Army-type shoulder straps, the infantry officer's color being black.

"The uniform coat for all enlisted men shall be a sack coat of gray cloth (of North Carolina manufacture) extending half way down the thigh, and made loose, with a falling collar, and an inside pocket on each breast, six coat buttons down the front, commencing at the throat; a strip of cloth sewed on each shoulder, extending from the base of the collar to the shoulder seam, an inch and a half wide at the base of the collar, and two inches wide at the shoulder; this strip will be of black cloth for Infantry, red for Artillery, and yellow for Cavalry.

"For a Musician... The same as for other enlisted men, with the addition of a bar of braid, horizontal to each button..." of branch-of-service color. Chevrons, also made in branch-of-service color, were to be the same as in the Confederate Army.

Trousers were the same color as coats, with a branch-of-service color welt down each leg for officers, and a buff welt for generals. All enlisted

1: Captain, S. Carolina, 1861
2: Cpl., Alabama Volunteer Corps, 1861
3: Pvt., 11th Mississippi Inf. Regt., 1861

A

1: Pvt., 2nd Rhode Island Inf. Regt., 1861
2: Sgt., 3rd Maine Vol. Regt., 1861
3: Pvt., 2nd New Hampshire Vol. Inf. Regt., 1861

B

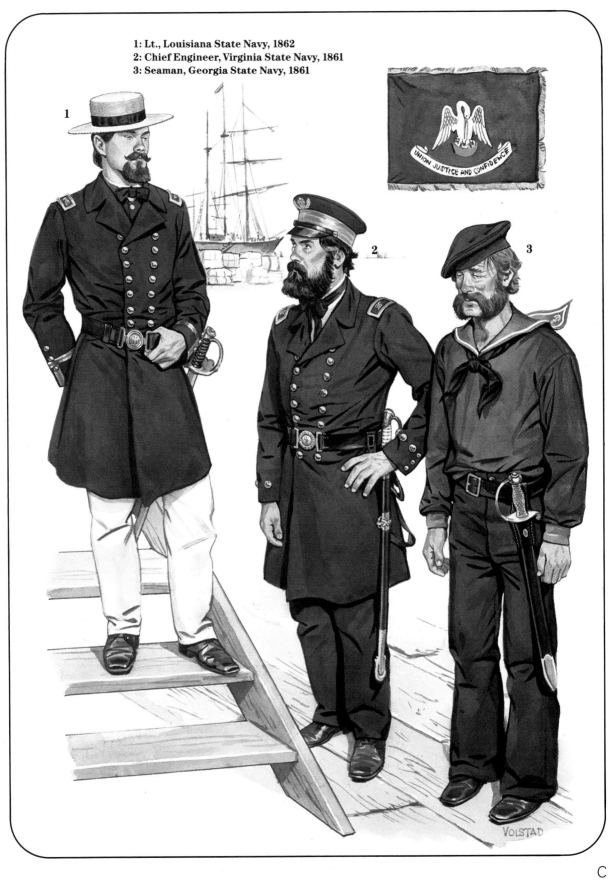

1: Lt., Louisiana State Navy, 1862
2: Chief Engineer, Virginia State Navy, 1861
3: Seaman, Georgia State Navy, 1861

UNION JUSTICE AND CONFIDENCE

VOLSTAD

C

1: Pvt., 10th Indiana Vol. Inf. Regt., 1861
2: 1st Sgt., 8th Wisconsin Vol. Inf. Regt., 1861
3: Pvt., Co.D, 7th Michigan Vol. Inf. Regt., 1861

D

1: Pvt., 1st Inf. Regt., Reserve Bde. of Philadelphia, 1863
2: Cpl., 33rd Pennsylvania Vol. Inf., 1862
3: Sgt., 1st Regt. Connecticut Militia, 1861

E

1: Ordinance Sgt., 3rd N. Carolina State Troops, 1863
2: Pvt., 7th Florida Vol. Inf. Regt., 1863
3: Sgt. Maj., 4th Georgia Inf. Regt., 1863

VOLSTAD

F

1: Pvt., 22nd NY State Militia Regt., 1863
2: 1st Lt., 69th NY State Militia Regt., 1862
3: Pvt., 33rd NY Vol. Inf. Regt., 1862

G

1: CQMS, 30th Ohio Vol. Inf. Regt., 1864
2: Pioneer, 17th Illinois Vol. Inf. Regt., 1863
3: RQMS, 3rd New Jersey Cav. Regt., 1864

H

men were to wear branch-of-service colored stripes down each leg, an inch wide for sergeants and regimental non-commissioned staff, ¾ in. for corporals, and ½ in. for privates.

Generals and general staff officers were to wear black felt hats "looped at the right side, with a large gilt button of the North Carolina pattern, and a gilt ornament in front, representing the Coat of Arms of North Carolina." Other officers wore the same hats in grey felt with US Army hat insignia in front. The same grey hats were worn by enlisted men with a branch-of-service color hat band, and a company letter and regimental number in front. "Officers, when off duty or on fatigue duty, may wear the French forage cap, according to pattern in Quarter Master General's office." Apparently, similar caps were also allowed to the men. All officers were to wear crimson silk sashes, while non-commissioned officers wore red worsted sashes.

There are enough surviving photographs and actual examples to indicate that the basic enlisted man's uniform, in some form at least, was worn throughout the war. Officers, after mid-1862 at any rate, seem to have followed Confederate Army regulations instead of state ones.

There were changes made in what the state issued from the beginning. In February 1862 it was decided to provide shell jackets instead of blouses (some blouses continued to be made up to the end of the war, however). These were to be made with shoulder straps and piped in branch-of-service colors.

After the state clothing factory was closed North Carolina began importing what its troops needed. Between June 1863 and the end of 1864 the state imported 50,000 blankets, grey wool for 250,000 uniforms, 12,000 overcoats, and either leather or ready-made shoes so that it had 250,000 pairs of shoes on hand. The state was so successful in providing for its men that when its warehouses were captured in April 1865 they still contained uniforms, shoes, and blankets for 92,000 men.

According to General Orders No. 1, the officers' sword belt plate was to be a "gilt, rectangle sword belt plate with North Carolina Coat of Arms on it." Enlisted men were to have a "belt plate after pattern in Quarter Master General's office" – although in reality the state issued few belt plates. A two-piece cast sword belt plate with the letters "NC" within a wreath is known, as is a similar plate with the state seal within its wreath.

This New York infantry private wears a state-issue jacket – too large, and folded up at the cuffs. His weapon is an M1842 smoothbore musket, and a revolver is stuck in his belt. (Richard Carlisle collection)

An oval, lead-backed US-type brass plate stamped "NC" in Roman letters is also known but this was apparently made before the war and is not commonly found at camp sites or battlefields. The 6th North Carolina Infantry Regiment had its own plates: cast brass ovals marked at the top "6TH INF" and at the bottom "NC.S.T." These plates appear to have had the background between the letters filled in with black enamel. They were found at 1862-63 camp sites.

While state belt plates are rare, state buttons are common. A three-piece stamped brass type has the state coat of arms in the center and "NORTH CAROLINA" around the outer top rim. The other common type was generally stamped copper with the shank soldered directly to the back; it featured the letters "NC" within a seven-pointed star burst.

North Carolina took immediate steps to get weapons into its troops' hands. In 1861 the state contracted M. A. Baker of Fayetteville to convert a large number of flintlock weapons – muskets, rifles, and muzzle-loading pistols – to percussion. These weapons were stamped "N. CAROLINA" on the barrel tops. The state then gave contracts to produce a weapon that was basically an M1841 "Mississippi" rifle with an M1855 nose cap to H. C. Lamb & Co. of Jamestown, who turned out 300 of these weapons per month between 1862 and 1865. A contract to produce 10,000 of the same weapon went to Mendenhall, Jones and Gardner of Whitsett.

OHIO

When the Civil War broke out Gen. Jacob D. Cox toured Ohio's state arsenal and found "a few boxes of smooth-bore muskets which had once been issued to militia companies and had been returned rusted and damaged. No belts, cartridge boxes, or other accoutrements were with them." Still, plans had to be made to handle the 10,000 expected volunteers. "There was no time to procure uniforms," Cox recalled, "nor was it desirable; for those companies had chosen their own, and would have to change it for that of the United States as soon as this could be furnished." Therefore, he wrote, "fancy uniforms were left at home, and some approximation to a simple and useful costume was made. The recent popular outburst in Italy furnished a useful idea, and the 'Garibaldi uniform' of a red flannel shirt with broad falling collar, with blue trousers held by a leathern waist-belt, and a soft [black] felt hat for the head, was extensively copied and served an excellent purpose. It could be made by the wives and sisters at home, and was all the more acceptable for that. The spring was opening and a heavy coat would not be much needed, so that with some sort of overcoat and a good blanket in an improvised knapsack, the new company was not badly provided."

So it was that most of Ohio's 1861 volunteers went to war in red flannel shirts, blue (sometimes grey) trousers, and black, broad-brimmed hats. Thereafter, the state planned to dress the volunteers in uniforms "so near that of the regular army, that no change would be required on going into the US service." The state went as far as to buy 8,000 regulation dress coats, complete with brass shoulder scales, to issue until the US government could take

The 65th New York Volunteer Infantry Regiment, also known as the 1st US Chasseurs and the 1st Grenadier Regiment, wore New York Chasseur jackets trimmed with light blue, and grey trousers. Their caps were made from issue caps with the peaks and chinstraps removed; the state seal was worn above the regimental number as a cap badge. This private holds one of the M1861 Springfield rifled muskets issued to the regiment; the leather gloves were not issue. (David Scheinmann collection)

over supply responsibilities, which happened in 1862. Until then, Ohio troops were to receive dark blue flannel shirts, sky blue trousers, and dark blue forage caps. Cavalry and light artillery were issued dark blue jackets trimmed in yellow and red respectively.

As it turned out, Ohio could not obtain enough blue wool, and grey uniforms had to be issued to a number of units instead. Grey jackets were made for 5,000 infantrymen, and were issued to – among others – the 15th, 17th, 19th, and 20th Ohio

Infantry Regiments. Grey trousers went to the 15th (which received grey striped trousers), 16th (also striped), 17th, 18th, 20th (also striped), and 22nd (also striped) Ohio Infantry Regiments. Grey overcoats went to the 16th Ohio Infantry, while the 21st and 22nd received black overcoats.

In April 1863 the state formed an "Ohio Volunteer Militia." This unit was to wear "the uniform prescribed for the United States Army for the time being, except the coat of arms, which shall be that of the State of Ohio."

The letters "OVM" appeared on a US Army-style oval brass belt plate and a cartridge box plate, worn not only by the Ohio Volunteer Militia of 1863 but also by early Ohio volunteer infantry regiments of 1861 and 1862. A circular shoulder belt plate with the insignia which became the state coat of arms, but otherwise like the US Army's eagle plate, was also worn by some volunteers in 1861. Sword belt plates were "gilt, rectangular, two inches wide, with a raised bright rim; a silver wreath encircling the arms of the state of Ohio," according to the 1859 *General Regulations for the Military Forces of Ohio*. There were, however, no special state buttons.

In 1861 Ohio acquired 15,020 M1842 muskets, 26,533 US-made muskets that had been converted from flintlock, 5,020 Prussian 0.72-cal. muskets, 11,480 P1858 Enfield rifled muskets, 4,991 0.69-cal. US-made muskets, and a couple of thousand other assorted types of muskets in small batches. These went to arm their initial infantry volunteers. Ohio also received 200 Joselyn carbines, 1,000 Sharps carbines, and 500 Colt army revolvers for her cavalry, along with 2,500 cavalry sabers. The Ohio Volunteer Militia received an equally odd mixture of longarms, ranging in caliber from 0.54 to 0.71.

PENNSYLVANIA

When, in May 1861, Pennsylvania's Quartermaster General began to let contracts for uniforms for the state's thousands of volunteers, there was no regulation state uniform to guide his contracts. His plan was to dress them all in blue; but this material was difficult to obtain, and grey uniforms were accepted for the emergency. Samples of swatches of material used, now preserved in the state's archives, vary from a drab or tan-grey,

A group of New York infantry privates, showing how the bottom front edges of the state-issue jacket were rounded. The two in the center hold their weapons at "shoulder arms," while the two on either side are in the position of "order arms." They wear a regimental number on their cap fronts. (David Scheinmann collection)

through cadet grey and light grey to dark grey. Some overcoat samples are dark grey with a very blue cast to them. Some "cadet satinet" samples for jackets are medium-dark; while other jacket samples, called "cadet mixed forest cloth," are actually light grey on one side and dark grey with a purplish cast on the other. Which side was to show on the outside is unknown.

The uniform produced with this material included, generally, a grey forage cap; plain grey trousers; and a plain, short jacket with a standing collar, keeper loops at each side to hold the waist belt, and nine to 12 buttons down the front. The state's Quartermaster also bought 13,000 pairs of "linen duck" trousers and "undress brown linen trousers," which were also widely issued. It is known, largely through photographs, that the following infantry regiments wore these grey uniforms when first organized: the 12th, 28th, 29th, and the 71st (trimmed with red). The 27th and 62nd Regiments may also have worn these grey uniforms.

Although these uniforms appear generally to have been replaced by the Peninsular Campaign of 1862, some Pennsylvanians continued to wear grey throughout the war. The Philadelphia Home Guard, for example, was to wear cadet

A typical camp scene of New Yorkers off duty. Note the tin cups, pots, and coffee kettles. A sergeant, standing left, watches the scene. (David Scheinmann collection)

grey uniforms, although, after April 24, 1861, a US Army dress hat could be substituted for the grey cadet cap. A grey frock coat and trousers were also worn by Philadelphia's Grey Reserves, although they did have blue fatigue uniforms for field wear.

At the same time, more Pennsylvanians volunteered than the US government was willing to accept into its service. Expecting a longer war than apparently foreseen by the War Department, the state's governor authorized the creation of a Pennsylvania Reserve Corps to take in these men, planning to turn them over to the US Army when needed. They were, in fact, eventually taken into the regular fighting army – confusing everyone ever since, because the units were numbered both with their reserve number and their regular volunteer state infantry regimental number!

The plan was that the PRC would "be armed and equipped, clothed...as similar troops in the service of the United States." As it turned out, the 1st (which became the 30th Pennsylvania Volunteer Infantry Regiment – the other PRC units taking numbers that followed in sequence), 2nd, 3rd, and 4th Reserves actually wore the state grey jackets, caps, and trousers when they were first mustered into service.

Pennsylvania put its state coat of arms on its buttons, but its belt plates were marked with unique designations by only a handful of militia or volunteer organizations, none of which saw any prolonged field service. These were generally brass oval plates like the US Army type, marked with unit designations like "PHG" (Philadelphia Home Guard), or "UAG" (Union Artillery Guard). The Reserve Brigade of Philadelphia had a similar plate, bearing the state coat of arms and the letters "RB." The US Army's belt plates were those most commonly used by Pennsylvanians, however. Most of the weapons used by Pennsylvania volunteers also came from the US government.

RHODE ISLAND

On April 18, 1861, the *Boston Daily Advertiser* reported "The following uniform has been selected for the Rhode Island Regiment – gray pantaloons, blue tunic, and a black felt hat with cockade and feathers." The "tunic" was actually a loose shirt worn outside the trousers. This was indeed the basic uniform adopted by the state in 1861 for all its volunteers. It was worn until late June 1862.

However, in September 1861 the state ordered that "the uniform of the Volunteers shall consist of a blue army cap, dark blue tunic and light blue pants" for its National Guard. This was apparently like the US fatigue dress, except that the tunic had five or sometimes six buttons instead of four. The US Army dress for officers was made regulation in June 1863. This was to include "a blue blouse, shoulder straps, dark pants, forage cap, sword and belt," in September 1863.

Rhode Island issued a button with its state coat of arms, but no other unique insignia. Weapons were largely received from the US government, apart from locally-produced Burnside carbines that were issued to both Rhode Island's cavalry and to several men in each company in the 1st Rhode Island Detached Militia Regiment.

Brigadier-General Jacob D. Cox, who was involved in the organization of Ohio's troops in 1861, wears the regulation uniform of the Ohio Volunteer Militia. It was the same as worn by regular US troops, in this case a dark blue frock coat with black velvet cuffs and standing collar, and a dark blue forage cap – though the latter bears the silver letters "OVM" in a gilt wreath. (David Scheinmann collection)

SOUTH CAROLINA

South Carolina's basic uniform regulations were written in 1839 and, while they were reprinted as late as 1860, they were fairly irrelevant to the Civil War period. New orders appeared in 1861 which brought them up to date for officers and senior non commissioned officers, at least, and imposed uniformity within South Carolina's military force.

Officers, according to the 1861 orders, were to wear dark blue frock coats and trousers like those of US Army officers. The trousers were to have a ½ in.-wide stripe for field officers and above, and an inch-wide stripe for company officers. Stripes were to be gold for generals and divisional and brigade staff officers; silver for field-grade officers and regimental staff; and white for company-grade officers. Coat buttons were to be gilt for generals and staff officers and silver for regimental officers. (In fact, all state buttons appear to have been gilt.)

Rank was indicated on the coats by gold or silver epaulettes, depending on the color of the wearer's buttons. The rank badges were the same as prescribed for US Army officers except that major-generals were to wear a silver crescent between two gold stars; brigadier-generals were to wear two silver stars; and colonels were to wear a gold Palmetto tree instead of an eagle. Staff non-commissioned officers were to wear the same dark blue uniform, with white worsted epaulettes to indicate their grade.

Hats varied. *Chapeaux de bras* were to be worn by field-grade officers and above for dress occasions. These were to be topped with a white ostrich feather tipped black for major-generals, and tipped red for brigadier-generals. Field-grade officers were to have a plain white cock feather. Company-grade officers had blue wool képis with a silver Palmetto tree badge in front, with the regimental number on the left as viewed, and the letter "R" on the right. This style of cap was to be worn in undress by all officers; however, generals and staff officers were to have a gold wreath surrounding the letters "SCV" as their cap badge, while field officers were to wear their regimental number within a silver wreath. Regimental staff officers wore the wreath around the letters "A" (for adjutant), "Q" (for quartermaster), "C" (for commissary), or "S" (for surgeon).

Despite these orders, grey became a more standard uniform almost immediately, at least for line troops. On January 25, 1861, the State Quartermaster advertised for "dark gray cloth, suitable for making uniforms for the troops." This

This private from Alliance, Ohio, wears the short jacket and black, broad-brimmed hat favored by Western soldiers. Note the watch chain just below the jacket bottom. (Author's collection)

was followed by an advertisement for bids for making 1,000 "plain frock coats and pantaloons of woolen" on February 18.

In actual practice, 1861 uniforms varied from company to company. According to the July 12, 1861, *Richmond Dispatch*, reporting the arrival of South Carolinians in that city, "as company after company came promptly into line, the gray dress of the 'Washingtons,' the darker hue of the 'Davis Guards,' the green, hunter-like, loose-fitting coat of the 'Gist Rifles,' together with the blue of the 'Bozeman Guards' and other shades of the 'Manning and Watson Guards' had a splendid effect." These uniforms quickly wore out, and issue Confederate uniforms became the norm thereafter.

Apparently preparing for war some years before 1861, the state ordered large numbers of stamped brass, lead-backed, US Army-type oval waist belt and cartridge box plates stamped "SC" in Roman letters. It even ordered circular, stamped brass, lead-backed shoulder belt plates bearing the state's palmetto device but otherwise like the US Army's eagle-design shoulder belt plates. Officers wore the usual two-piece, cast brass plates with the state coat of arms on the male part, as well as several types of rectangular cast brass belt plates with the same design. The state's buttons bearing its coat of arms also appear to have been made largely by Northern companies like H. & G. Schuyler, New York, before the war.

The state launched a major program to arm itself during the years before the war. In 1851 it contracted with William Glaze and Benjamin Flagg to set up the Palmetto Armory in Colombia to make 6,000 M1842 muskets (6,020 were actually produced), 2,000 M1842 single-shot pistols, 1,000 M1840 cavalry sabers, 1,000 M1841 rifles, and 1,000 artillery swords. These were to come "with their equipment complete."

TENNESSEE

Tennessee's Union troops wore standard US Army uniforms, while their Confederate troops wore standard dress for their army. There does not appear to have been a state belt plate, although it has been suggested that a very crude rectangular stamped copper belt plate marked "VS" and found in a Southern site may represent the

"Volunteer State," Tennessee's motto. Buttons bearing the Tennessee coat of arms were worn by state troops on both sides.

Tennessee's Southern troops were also badly armed. As late as April 1, 1862, the 55th Tennessee Infantry Regiment was reported as having only a few weapons, and those of various makes. The 46th Infantry had "only two companies armed (400 for duty, 160 armed)." A report from the Department of East Tennessee on April 25, 1862, indicates that the state's Southern infantry regiments were badly armed, mostly with "country rifles." The 1st Infantry Battalion was unarmed, while the 2nd, 3rd, and 8th Cavalry Battalions were "partly and badly armed with shotguns."

TEXAS

"When my regiment was organized that spring," wrote 4th Texas Infantry Regiment Pvt. Val C. Giles, "there were no two companies who had uniforms alike. It was some time after the war began before the Confederacy adopted any particular style of uniform. The color was universally gray, but the cut of cloth varied considerably. We were a motley-looking set, but as a rule, comfortably dressed. In my company we had about four different shades of gray, but the trimmings were all of black braid."

Photographs of men of the 1st Infantry Regiment taken in early 1862 near Richmond show mostly frock coats, some with stripes across the chest like those sported by Mississippi troops. Most have cadet-pattern forage caps with regimental designations spelled out on their crowns in what appear to be brass letters.

Texas troops who stayed West seemed to prefer Western, civilian-type dress. Pvt. Dunnie Affleck, Co. B, Terry's Texas Rangers, wrote home on March 25, 1863: "Mexican hats, and buckskin suits are the fashion amongst the Rangers now, nearly all are sending for them, and I want to keep in fashion." He also wanted some checkered shirts.

Cut off from Eastern supplies after the fall of Vicksburg, the state set up its Lone Star Mill at the Huntsville Penitentiary. There they produced vast quantities of jeans materials for uniforms, probably mostly grey-colored.

The state also issued pre-war oval, stamped brass, US-type belt plates (but no cartridge box plates) bearing a five-pointed star in the center. These came in two styles, one flat and one with the center of the star raised: it is possible that the first style was not actually used during the war. Rectangular belt plates bearing the star design were also used, as were two-piece swordbelt plates with the star within the wreath. Texas buttons also bore a star, with the word "TEXAS" around its points.

On January 11, 1862, Texas set up a military board to buy weapons, and subsequently even set up its own cannon foundry. Copies of a Colt Dragoon

A private of the 126th Pennsylvania Volunteer Infantry Regiment, a regiment raised for nine months' service in 1862. He wears the dark blue shell jacket and trousers issued by the state to this regiment. According to Brigadier-General Erastus B. Tylor, at the Battle of Chancellorsville "for earnest, spirited work [the 126th] could not be excelled." (Author's collection) model revolver were made for the state by Tucker & Sherrard of Lancaster, who had a contract for 3,000 revolvers but only produced some 400. Dance Brothers of Galveston also produced some 300 copies of the Colt Navy revolver for the state. Although made for the Confederate government, many rifles produced at the Tyler, Texas Armory ended up in the hands of Texans.

VERMONT

There were no Vermont-wide dress regulations, so when the 1st Volunteer Infantry Regiment was raised in 1861 the Quartermaster General simply chose grey as a popular and easy-to-acquire uniform color. He ordered grey uniforms for the regiment, with coats made with tails, and overcoats like those used in Massachusetts. For the 2nd and 3rd Regiments, however, he contracted a local company to make brownish-grey frock coats, trousers and caps, all piped with blue cord, and fastened with state buttons. Regiments were clothed thereafter by the US Army in regulation blue. Frock coats were apparently preferred by Vermonters to fatigue shirts, even for field use.

The state button bore the coat of arms under "VERMONT." This was the only state-wide special insignia, although the 13th Infantry Regiment wore its number within a brass wreath on its cap tops; the 4th Infantry Band wore a large number "4," apparently in light blue, on each left coat breast; and the 1st to 6th Infantry Regiments wore hemlock sprigs within their forage cap chinstraps.

Vermont was able to provide M1855 Springfields for the 1st Infantry Regiment; M1842 muskets for the 2nd, and P1858 Enfields for the 3rd. Higher-numbered regiments were armed by the US government.

VIRGINIA

On March 2, 1858, Virginia issued dress regulations that were virtually the same as those of the US Army, except for insignia on buttons and cap badges. However, volunteer companies were allowed to continue wearing their old, distinctive uniforms, and it was in these that most of the state's troops went to war. The state's volunteers included 79 companies of "Grays," the most popular color, and

This stamped brass oval belt plate, the back filled with lead, bears the state seal of Pennsylvania and the letters "RB," for the Reserve Brigade of Philadelphia. The plate is typical of the state seal-issued belt plates which were the same size as the US Army issue type. (Author's collection)

14 of "Blues," despite the fact that the 1858 orders made blue the state color. Generally, grey frock coats, trousers, and French-style képis, all trimmed with colored braid (often black), represented the most popular uniform. A number of cavalry units wore grey shirts as their field dress.

Virginia also set up a state navy, and ordered on April 25, 1861, that "The uniform of the Officers, Seamen and Marines of the Virginia Navy shall correspond in all respects to that of the United States Navy, with the exception of the BUTTON, which shall be that of the Commonwealth of Virginia." This force was merged into the Confederate Navy when that organization was formed.

For its land forces' shoulder belts and waist belts, Virginia issued 57,912 yards of white webbing between October 1, 1859, and November 1, 1861. The state also issued 2,079 leather waist belts during the same period, as well as 9,630 shoulder belt plates. Some of these were basically the same as the US Army eagle plate, but bore the state coat of arms. Plain cast brass circular plates appear to have been more common, however. No such plates were issued after November 1861.

Virginia also issued, during the same period, 12,916 waist belt plates, followed by another 364 issued during the entire following year. These may have been cast brass rectangular plates bearing the state coat of arms: this type of plate appears, from digging at various sites, to have been fairly common.

Another variation simply had the word "VIRGINIA" within a wreath. Up to November 1861 the state issued 20,136 cartridge boxes but only 1,341 box plates, probably of the US Army type. The following year 5,271 cartridge boxes were issued, but no plates. Some 3,852 sword belt plates were issued up to November 1861: these were two-piece, brass, with the state seal within a wreath. The 1st Virginia Infantry Regiment wore an oval cast brass plate with the unit designation engraved on it, and brought up to date by adding the letters "C.S.A." in the center. The 3rd Virginia Infantry wore a rectangular belt plate with the unit designation engraved on it.

Virginia had 50,000 old state-manufactured flintlocks in 1861, and it rapidly contracted six Richmond gunsmiths to convert these to percussion. (Some 58,428 of these weapons had been made very early in the 19th century.) In addition, the first weapons produced on the captured Harper's Ferry Armory rifled musket machinery went to Virginia.

WISCONSIN

Wisconsin's officers were to wear US Army uniforms after 1858, but, as in so many Northern states, there was not enough blue material for all its volunteers at the outbreak of war. The state's 1st and 2nd Infantry Regiments therefore wore plain, single-breasted grey frock coats, grey trousers with a black cord down each leg, a grey képi trimmed with black, and a grey overcoat with black piping on cuffs and pockets. The 3rd's uniforms included dark grey hunting shirts or frocks, light grey trousers, and grey broad-brimmed hats turned up on one side.

Thereafter, standard uniforms were made for the 4th to 8th Infantry Regiments. These included grey single-breasted jackets with black shoulder straps and black trim on the collars and cuffs (except for the 5th, which had only cuff trim). They had grey keeper loops on each side, buttoned at the top, through which the waistbelts were to pass. Plain grey forage caps, grey trousers with a black cord down each leg, and grey overcoats completed this uniform. Much of the material used was of poor quality. Blue drilling overalls had to be issued almost immediately to the 1st and 3rd Infantry Regiments because their grey trousers wore out so quickly.

By February 1862 all the state's volunteers were wearing blue uniforms. These were not US regulation uniforms, however, for the state issued the 9th to 16th Infantry Regiments dark blue sack coats, made with a standing collar edged with sky blue and with five buttons down the front. Black broad-brimmed hats were issued as well as blue forage caps. Trousers were sky blue. Regiments thereafter received US regulation dress.

Wisconsin had a unique button displaying its state coat of arms which was used in the 4th to 16th Infantry Regiments – the US general service button was used in the other units. There was no state belt plate.

The longarms issued by the state included a mixture of largely foreign-made weapons (mostly listed as "Garibaldi rifle muskets, caliber .71").

Private A. M. Grant, Landis' Philadelphia Battery of Light Artillery, was photographed in that city just after the battery's return from the Gettysburg campaign – the mud of the campaign is still visible on his trouser legs. The battery skirmished with J. E. B. Stuart's cavalry near Carlisle, Pennsylvania, during that campaign. Its dress included a light drab slouch hat, with a red cord and crossed brass cannon under the letter "A": dark blue fatigue shirt and trousers (the shirt having five buttons down the front); and a two-piece 1835 belt plate. (Author's collection)

SELECT BIBLIOGRAPHY

Alphaeus H. Albert, *Record of American Uniform and Historical Buttons*, Boyertown, Pennsylvania, 1976

William G. Gavin, *Accoutrement Plates North and South 1861–1865*, Philadelphia, 1963

John Niven, *Connecticut for the Union*, New Haven, Connecticut, 1965

Frederick P. Todd, *American Military Equippage 1851–1872*, Volume II, New York, 1983

THE PLATES

A1: CAPTAIN, SOUTH CAROLINA, 1861

The dark blue uniform worn by this staff captain is described by British correspondent William H. Russell on April 17, 1861, as "blue military caps, with 'palmetto' trees embroidered thereon, blue frock-coats, with upright collars, and shoulder-straps edged with lace, and marked with two silver bars, to designate their ranks of captain; gilt buttons with the palmetto in relief; blue trowsers, with a goldlace cord, and brass spurs – no straps."

A2: CORPORAL, ALABAMA VOLUNTEER CORPS, 1861

The state uniform, with minor variations from unit to unit, was worn at least into 1863. This corporal is armed with an M1842 smoothbore 0.69-cal. musket; the bayonet scabbard is the M1840 model which was designed for this musket.

A3: PRIVATE, 11TH MISSISSIPPI INFANTRY REGIMENT, 1861

Photographs indicate that the 11th Mississippi, as well as a large number of other state infantry regiments, wore the basic state uniform, at least in 1861. This private's belt plate bears the state insignia. Hat brims were folded up according to individual or unit taste on one or both sides, and sometimes to even form tricornes. The 11th, then part of Hood's Division, defended the part of the Southern line near the Dunker Church at the Battle of Antietam. Charged again and again, they lost 104 killed or wounded in the action, including all their field officers; but they held their line.

B1: PRIVATE, 2ND RHODE ISLAND INFANTRY REGIMENT, 1861

Rhode Island's state uniform was loose and comfortable: basically a blue hunting shirt – a garment with a long military tradition in America. A type of Mexican *serape* was also worn over the shirt in cooler weather. The regiment had switched to the regulation uniform when, as part of the VI Corps at Spotsylvania in 1864, they were in the center of the brigade sent to hold part of the captured lines. Four

Colonel Ambrose Burnside wears the field-grade officers' version of the Rhode Island dark blue frock. It has two rows of brass buttons down the front, while that of company-grade officers and enlisted men had only one row of buttons. His trousers are grey. (David Scheinmann collection)

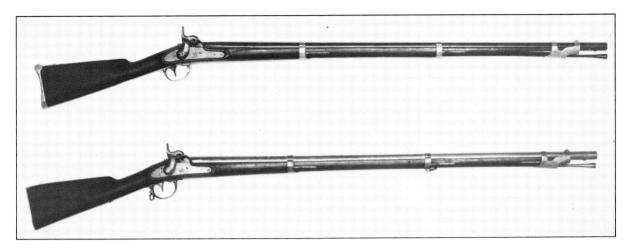

South Carolina bought copies of the M1842 musket from two makers, A. H. Waters & Co. (*top*), and B. Flagg & Co. (*bottom*). The state bought about 100 of the Waters musket in 1849, and 640 of the Flagg weapons in 1850. The Waters has brass furniture, the Flagg iron furniture. (Milwaukee Public Museum)

times they were assaulted, and on the last occasion the Confederates even managed to plant a flag on their works. But four times they held – even though their guns were so fouled that they could no longer be loaded, and had to be exchanged for fresh ones.

B2: SERGEANT, 3RD MAINE VOLUNTEER INFANTRY REGIMENT, 1861

The 3rd Maine received state-produced grey uniforms, as well as distinctive tin drum-type canteens, and state insignia belt plates. These uniforms were of poor material though, so were replaced when the regiment reached the front with US Army regulation dress. (The belt plates and canteens were retained.) The 3rd had its roughest day on July 2, 1863, at Gettysburg, where they were first sent as a skirmish line in support of the US Sharpshooters in front of the II Corps; and were then ordered to rejoin the III Corps in the Peach Orchard, where they were battered by repeated attacks. They entered the battle with 14 officers and 196 enlisted men; they lost 113 all ranks during that day, along with their national color.

B3: PRIVATE, 2ND NEW HAMPSHIRE VOLUNTEER INFANTRY REGIMENT, 1861

Two novel items are worn by this private of the 2nd New Hampshire: the "Whipple" hat and "camp shoes." The Whipple hat was widely issued to troops from New Hampshire, New York, and Massachusetts. It is often incorrectly shown in modern drawings based on vague period engravings as a type of pith helmet, but it was actually made of blue felt with a leather peak and chinstrap. These caps were worn at least until mid-1862, and were highly popular, when captured, among

Confederates, who called them "Excelsior" hats (after New York's motto). The camp shoes were worn throughout the war, and were made of white canvas, with leather ties, toes, and heels. This private also wears the state grey uniform and unique belt plate.

The 2nd was in the III Corps at Gettysburg, posted in the Peach Orchard behind the 3rd Maine on July 2. The 3rd Maine withdrew and, to defend their position, the 2nd charged the attacking Southern line and drove them back. In turn, however, they were forced back under heavy fire, retiring, reported their colonel, "quite rapidly, yet coolly, and without excitement as they went." The 2nd New Hampshire lost 193 all ranks during the day.

C1: LIEUTENANT, LOUISIANA STATE NAVY, 1862

Louisiana's Navy fought unsuccessfully against the US Navy below New Orleans. The officers were described in US Navy officers' uniforms, such as this one worn by a lieutenant, with white trousers and a straw hat – also worn in the US Navy – for hot weather. His sword belt plate bears the state insignia, while his sword was made by L. Haiman & Bros., of Columbus, Georgia, for officers of the Confederate Navy.

C2: CHIEF ENGINEER, VIRGINIA STATE NAVY, 1861

Officers in the Virginia Navy wore US Navy uniforms, with the exception of the state insignia on

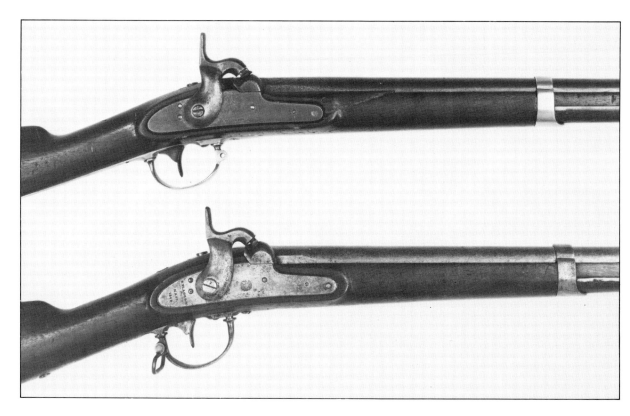

Lockplates of the A. H. Waters & Co. M1842 musket (*top*) and the B. Flagg & Co. M1842 musket (*bottom*). (Milwaukee Public Museum)

their buttons and sword belt plates. This engineer's branch is indicated by his unique cap badge and shoulder straps, while the three buttons around his cuff indicate his rank. His sword is the US Navy officer's model.

C3: SEAMAN, GEORGIA STATE NAVY, 1861

Georgia's Navy lasted only a matter of months, yet in that time a receiving ship had been set up and men enlisted into it. This sailor wears the rather unique dress prescribed for that force, and is armed with a cutlass made by Cook & Brother in New Orleans, Louisiana.

D1: PRIVATE, 10TH INDIANA VOLUNTEER INFANTRY REGIMENT, 1861

All Indiana's first six regiments wore a version of this basic uniform, some in grey and some in blue. Made of lightweight satinet, these uniforms wore out rapidly and were later replaced with regulation US Army dress. At the Battle of Logan's Cross Roads in January 1862, which saved Kentucky for the Union, the 10th were attacked and fell back, but

rallied and moved to the front again to cover an exposed flank. Running out of ammunition and refilling their cartridge boxes while still under fire, they then charged and broke the Confederate line, which was never rallied again for the rest of the battle.

D2: FIRST SERGEANT, 8TH WISCONSIN VOLUNTEER INFANTRY REGIMENT, 1861

The 8th Wisconsin was the last of the state's regiments to receive grey uniforms. The 8th, which served in Western campaigns including that against Vicksburg in 1863, was best known for its mascot, "Old Abe," an American eagle that was noted for flying low over its ranks in battle, giving a mournful cry. This first sergeant is armed with a P1858 Enfield rifled musket from England.

D3: PRIVATE, CO. D, 7TH MICHIGAN VOLUNTEER INFANTRY REGIMENT, 1861

Although Michigan ordered blue uniforms from the first day it began to get supplies for its volunteers, a number of pre-war or homemade uniforms appeared when the troops first mustered. This outfit was initially worn by the Monroe Light Guard which became Co. D of the 7th Infantry; it did not last long in service, however. The state uniforms were of similar designs, but all dark blue. When the Union Army was held up by snipers inside houses in Fredericksburg, and artillery failed to dislodge them, the 7th jumped into pontoons along with troops from the 19th and 20th Massachusetts Regiments, and crossed the river, to drive the Confederates out of the town. This allowed the engineers to get on with the job of assembling the pontoon bridges so that the rest of the Army could cross to the disastrous Battle of Fredericksburg.

E1: PRIVATE, 1ST INFANTRY REGIMENT, RESERVE BRIGADE OF PHILADELPHIA, 1863

Pennsylvania's Reserve Brigade, organized in April 1861, continued to wear grey uniforms long after all the other Federal volunteers at the front switched to blue. When the regiment saw field duty, however, in the southern invasions of 1862 and 1863, and came under artillery fire at Carlisle, Pennsylvania, they wore dark blue fatigue blouses. Their belt plates were unique, with the state coat of arms over the letters "RB."

E2: CORPORAL, 33RD PENNSYLVANIA VOLUNTEER INFANTRY, 1862

The state's first generally issued uniform was this simple grey affair, worn at least until mid-1862. This corporal holds the regimental color, like the US flag but with the state coat of arms in the canton along with the stars. Each of the state's regiments received one of these colors, which differed only in very minor points. At 2nd Bull Run the 33rd charged down the slope of Henry House Hill, taking up a defensive line on the Sudley Springs Road, and driving every Confederate from their front. According to Gen. George Meade, "it is due to the Pennsylvania Reserves to say this charge and maintenance was made at a most critical period of the day." The Union Army's defeat could well have been much worse had it not been made.

E3: SERGEANT, 1ST REGIMENT OF CONNECTICUT MILITIA, 1861

Companies A and B of Connecticut's infantry regiments were rifle companies, trimming their uniforms with green. This uniform was authorized by state regulations before the war, and closely followed that of the US Army's 1858 regulations, replacing national insignia with state insignia. His canteen is a unique combination of canteen and ration carrier, issued to several 1861 Connecticut volunteer regiments: the top part holds water, while the hollow bottom part is designed for rations. The 1st, which served only three months in 1861, were at 1st Bull Run where, after crossing the stream following Sherman's Brigade, they marched down Young's Branch and were pretty well out of the fighting for the rest of the day.

F1: ORDNANCE SERGEANT, 3RD NORTH CAROLINA STATE TROOPS, 1863

This ordnance sergeant holds the regimental color, a dangerous privilege that seems often to have fallen to ordnance sergeants in North Carolina units. He wears the regulation state uniform, with the pre-war state belt plate. His canteen is made of two pieces of shaped wood nailed together. The 3rd was in the lead in the famous flank march made by "Stonewall" Jackson at Chancellorsville.

Texas bought these tin canteens from Kirschbaum of Solingen in Prussia. Alabama bought identically marked canteens, which were, however, made of copper instead of tin. (Don Johnson collection)

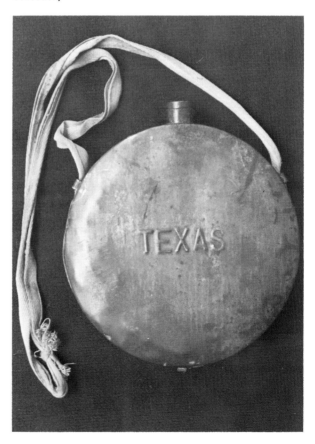

Vermonters, like this private from Chelsea, Vermont, wore US regulation frock coats even in the field. His cap is marked with a branch-of-service infantry insignia with a company letter "G" within the horn loop. (Author's collection)

F2: PRIVATE, 7TH FLORIDA VOLUNTEER INFANTRY REGIMENT, 1863

Florida did issue some uniforms to its troops, including this 7th Infantry private. The jacket and trousers were lightweight, made with cotton rather than wool. His canteen is a copper copy of the US Army tin canteen. The 7th, in Finley's Brigade of Bate's Division of the Army of the Tennessee, served in the defense of Atlanta.

F3: SERGEANT MAJOR, 4TH GEORGIA INFANTRY REGIMENT, 1863

This sergeant major wears a common variation of the regulation chevrons for his grade. He also wears a belt plate with the state insignia; and his wooden canteen is taken from one carried by a member of Co. G of this regiment. The 4th was one of the regiments that fought the delaying action at South Mountain, thus preventing the Union Army from destroying the Army of Northern Virginia piecemeal.

G1: PRIVATE, 22ND NEW YORK STATE MILITIA REGIMENT, 1863

New York's state militia was not the same as her volunteer regiments at the front – something that can be confusing, since the same numbers were used by pairs of quite distinct regiments. Most state militia units wore uniforms that they designed for themselves and were not in state-wide use. The 22nd, a New York City regiment, preferred grey uniforms; the state insignia was worn on the cap box and buttons, while the company letter appeared on the cap front and belt plate. The regiment was made part of the New York National Guard in September 1861. It served at Harper's Ferry, Virginia, in June 1862, at which time it returned its grey uniforms and donned blue fatigue shirts, because the grey ones were too similar to Confederate ones. They were armed with sergeants' P1856 Enfield rifles.

G2: FIRST LIEUTENANT, 69TH NEW YORK STATE MILITIA REGIMENT, 1862

The 69th Volunteer Infantry and 69th State Militia Regiments were closely associated – both were Irish units from New York City – with 500 officers and men from the State Militia Regiment volunteering for service in the Volunteer Infantry Regiment when it was organized. This figure is based closely on a photograph of the State Militia's First Lieutenant E. K. Butler, which shows him to have carried a silver flask as a canteen. His belt plate is the state sword belt plate. The color in the background was carried by the 69th Volunteer Infantry until late 1862. At 1st Bull Run the State Militia regiment successfully attacked the 4th Alabama, its lieutenant-colonel being killed in the process. The Volunteer Infantry Regiment was part of the famous "Irish Brigade" of the Army of the Potomac, who smashed into the Confederate line in the Sunken Lane at Antietam in September 1862 despite terrible losses.

G3: PRIVATE, 33RD NEW YORK VOLUNTEER INFANTRY REGIMENT, 1862

The 33rd was one of the many New York infantry units that received the state uniform jacket. They also wore the state belt plates. This was the typical uniform of the majority of New York's infantrymen. The 33rd was the last regiment in the rearguard when the Union army changed bases during the Peninsular Campaign. On June 28, 1862, when so serving, it was attacked by the 7th and 8th Georgia Regiments. The 33rd checked the attack, capturing 50 prisoners including both Georgia colonels, and finding another 100 Southerners wounded or dead in front of their position.

H1: COMPANY QUARTERMASTER SERGEANT, 30TH OHIO VOLUNTEER INFANTRY REGIMENT, 1864

Ohio's troops, typical of many Westerners, were often issued short jackets instead of fatigue shirts or frock coats. This man wears a half-chevron indicating veteran volunteer status. His cross belt plate bears the state insignia, and he also wears the state belt plate. At the Battle of South Mountain the 30th charged into the 23rd North Carolina Infantry, who were positioned behind a stone wall. "Some of the 30th Ohio forced through a breach in the wall," Confederate Gen. D. H. Hill wrote later, "and bayonets and clubbed muskets were used freely for a few moments." They drove the North Carolinians off and took the position.

H2: PIONEER, 17TH ILLINOIS VOLUNTEER INFANTRY REGIMENT, 1863

The pioneers' grade is indicated by the crossed ax insignia worn on both sleeves. This regiment, when photographed near Vicksburg, Mississippi, in 1863, wore state-issued jackets and broad-brimmed hats. At the Battle of Shiloh, "left unsupported and alone…the 17th Illinois…retired in good order…and reformed under my direction," reported Union Gen. McClernand. This calm behavior, which was not typical of many of the units first hit by the Southern assault, helped save the day, and the campaign in the West, for the Union.

H3: REGIMENTAL QUARTERMASTER SERGEANT, 3RD NEW JERSEY CAVALRY REGIMENT, 1864

When the 3rd New Jersey Cavalry was raised in January–March 1864, the state decided to name them the "1st US Hussars" and to give them a fancier than usual cavalry uniform, as a spur to recruitment. The state paid for the additions to the regulation cavalry uniform. The cap was the issue forage cap with the peak removed and worn sideways (although the crossed sabers insignia on top of the cap was worn facing the original front). Extra braid was added to the jackets. Called the "Butterflies" by other troops when they first appeared, the regiment went on to establish a credible record as a good cavalry unit. Their most notable action was their charge to capture the

This corporal from Madison, Wisconsin, wears a version of that state's grey uniform with black trim on the trousers and jacket cuffs and collar. The shirt is made without a collar, and is apparently dark blue or red with a light-colored piped design down the front. (Richard Carlisle collection)

entire 8th South Carolina Infantry Regiment, but they also made a successful charge at Winchester, Virginia; routed Southern cavalry at Tom's Brook, Virginia; and were at the Battle of Five Forks.

INDEX

(References to illustrations are shown in **bold**. Plates are shown with caption locators in brackets.)